A BASKET

OF

BARLEY LOAVES.

BY THE

AUTHOR OF "THE HIGH MOUNTAIN APART" AND "SACRAMENTAL SABBATHS."

"There is a lad here, which hath five barley loaves."—JOHN vi. 9.

PHILADELPHIA:
PRESBYTERIAN BOARD OF PUBLICATION,
No. 1334 CHESTNUT STREET.

WESTCOTT & THOMSON,
Stereotypers, Philada.

TO

MY FORMER PASTOR,

REV. ALEXANDER DICKSON,

WHO TAUGHT ME

"THE WAY OF GOD MORE PERFECTLY,"

AND WHOSE THOUGHTS AND VERY WORDS ENTER LARGELY INTO THESE PAGES,

I DEDICATE THIS

BASKET OF BARLEY LOAVES.

EDITOR'S PREFACE.

To those who crave more of Christ in the soul and in the daily life, to those who long for holiness and assurance, this BASKET OF BARLEY LOAVES will bring welcome refreshment and nourishment. The devout, even though trembling, believer, who hungers after righteousness, will here find that which will kindle his affections and lead them to the only satisfying source of love and peace, Jesus Christ. What of sweetness and strength there is in these meditations is due to God's word, of which they are full. Sweeter than honey and the honey-comb, more precious than silver or gold, was that word to the Psalmist; and thence these chapters draw their flavor and force. By them the weary, the needy, the longing, will be led nearer to Christ and be more filled with the power of his love. May these few Barley Loaves feed many thousands of hungry souls!

J. W. D.

CONTENTS.

XVI.

XVII.

XVIII.

XIX.

A BASKET
OF
BARLEY LOAVES.

I.

Jesus Sought and Found.

THE crowd was thronging and jostling. Eager and wistful faces were turned to One who stood in the midst. His countenance was mild and compassionate; and as I gazed upon him, a deep desire filled my heart to know and follow this Man of Sorrows. With swiftest steps I hurried on and pressed into the crowd. The lowly, suffering woman was satisfied to touch the hem of his garments, and it was enough. But

I was not content until I had grasped his hand. Yes, I put my hand in his—my guilty hand that nailed him to the cross.

"Who touched me?" He turned, and we stood face to face. In answer to his inquiry I whispered, "Lord, I will follow thee whithersoever thou goest." A look of love glanced from his eye; nearer he drew me to his side and whispered, "Beloved." Oh how it thrilled my heart! Excess of joy choked my utterance, and I could only grasp his hand more firmly and exclaim, "My Lord and my God!"

Tell me not now of loneliness and desolation. Jesus is mine, and so we journey hand in hand; and as he whispers to me of love unchangeable, I hide this sweet secret in my heart and answer, "I am thine."

"They tell me," we said to an aged man, "that you have no rock on which to plant your feet." "No rock?" he said, calmly, with a smile—"no rock? Well, my creed does differ from yours. Mine is love to

God and love to my fellow-men. I do not believe such a man as Jesus Christ ever lived. The world has had many saviours. Mine is a principle—a rightening principle. I have tried all beliefs, and here I am content to rest."

But we have not so learned Christ.

Infidels may tell me such a man never lived; humanitarians may tell me he was mere man and no God; careless worldlings may tell me there is no beauty in him that I should desire him; but from the far-off region of light, beyond the mist-clouds that encircle the earth, I hear a voice, calm in its majesty and tender in its tones: "I am Alpha and Omega, the beginning and the ending, saith the Lord, which is, and which was, and which is to come, the Almighty." "I am the light of the world: he that followeth me shall not walk in darkness, but shall have the light of life." "I am the Lord thy God, the Holy One of Israel, thy Saviour." "I, even I, am the

Lord; and beside me there is no Saviour." "O Israel, thou hast destroyed thyself, but in me is thine help." "I will ransom them from the power of the grave; I will redeem them from death." "Come unto me, all ye that labor and are heavy laden, and I will give you rest."

Hearing this voice I draw nearer. "Have I been so long time with you, and yet hast thou not known me? Thou hast both seen him, and he it is that talketh with thee." "Lord, I believe." "I know thee who thou art, the Holy One of God." With the eye of faith I have seen thee, and I can testify that "thou art fairer than the children of men." With the hand of faith I have grasped thine, O thou Friend that stickest closer than a brother." And thou hast talked with me. "Never man spake like this man." I cannot utter half the words Jesus has spoken to my soul; but this I say: Into his hands I commit my soul with all its interests; "for I know whom I have believed, and am persuaded that he is able to keep that which I have committed unto him against that day."

"O Jesus, Friend unfailing,
How dear thou art to me!
And, cares or fears assailing,
I find my strength in thee.

"I love to own, Lord Jesus,
Thy claims o'er me and mine;
Bought with thy blood most precious,
Whose can I be but *thine?*"

"As the late lamented Dudley Tyng was passing from the earthly vineyard to his higher position in the heavenly," writes Boardman in his book entitled "Him that Overcometh," "he said to his father, while light fell upon him from the open gateway, 'Father, stand up for Jesus.' Then, after advancing a little farther on into the fuller effulgence, he spoke again, saying, 'Father, stand up in Jesus.' These injunctions were reported by his father as they fell from the lips of his son, and went abroad all over the land. The first one struck a chord which vibrates still, and passed into a watchword for all Christian enterprise and for all enterprising Christians, but the second seemed to find no chord keyed up and ready to respond. It is to be feared that this is indicative of the true state of the Christian world to-day—*for* Christ, more than *in* him; and yet, if we may believe the words of Christ himself, and the history of all the progress of his kingdom, we have the secret of all power in these two words, "in Jesus," with the converse of them, "Jesus in us."

"*Abide in me, and I in you.*" Christ within is better even than Christ beside us, as the apostles found after Pentecost. This is the secret of all joy and the source of all strength.

To those who are just starting on the Christian pilgrimage we would repeat these words of the Master, "Abide in me." Guide-books are good, but a trusty guide is better. We might fill our pages with minute directions concerning the way, but we would rather point to Christ, who is the way. We remember that there are times when travelers forget their guide-books and cling to their strong and sure-footed guides.

Consider our Guide. He knows every step of the way, and he will guide us with his eye. Let us meditate upon Christ till our hearts are led to desire more intimate fellowship with him. "My meditation of him shall be sweet"—"sweet" when I remember his name, his character, his work, his promises and the peace he gives.

But it may be that some to whom these pages are addressed find many dark threads of doubt woven into their meditation of Christ. You have never, perhaps, been fully assured of your acceptance with him; or, if confident at the commencement of your Christian course, doubts and fears may have gathered around your pathway before journeying very far into the wilderness. The chilling winds of unbelief make winter in your soul. The days are short and cold; the nights are long and colder. Yes, even the day seems as the night—all darkness. Some around you seem to be enjoying perpetual spring-time, because Christ shines so constantly upon their happy souls, and your coldness and darkness seem all the sadder in contrast with their warmth and brightness.

How can you account for this? Ask some Christian friends, and they will tell you that you must not expect so much joy—that the Christian life is a constant conflict with doubt and sin, and you cannot expect to be always as happy as perhaps you were at first. You turn away sadly disappointed. They are older Christians, and you think they must know better than you. What will you do? Will you sit under the clouds, or struggle to get out into clear sunshine?

We cannot think that God intends you to

have a limited measure of joy and peace. Why should you not grow happier in your love to Christ as you learn to know him better? Why should not the promises become more precious as you prove them and find them all "yea and amen in Christ Jesus?"

Let us inquire into the cause of your darkness. The Saviour does not willingly withhold his smile which makes spring and summer in the soul. When God made a covenant with you he gave you this promise: "I will never leave thee, nor forsake thee." God has not then forsaken you. Perhaps you have neglected the means of grace. Perhaps you are cherishing some secret sin. Perhaps you have looked more to your own frames and feelings than to Christ's perfect work. Your mind has dwelt too much upon self. Take the advice of one who walked with God and was not, because God took him: "For one look at self take ten looks to Christ." The advice is good, and it has lifted many a Christian above the clouds.

"Saw ye Him whom my soul loveth? I sought him, but I found him not." Is this your sad lament?

Seek him again. Seek him earnestly, prayerfully, constantly. Seek him in the place of secret prayer. Jesus had his secret place upon the lonely mountain. Though he lived in constant communion with his Father, though his every step was a hymn of praise and his every act was a prayer, still he felt his need of a place where he could pour out his soul in supplication. If secret prayer was necessary for the Master, is it not more needful for you? If you have neglected that, it is not strange if it is winter in your soul.

Seek Jesus also in his holy word. In the garden of the gospel you may meet him and walk with him, holding sweet communion. Here he reveals himself. Obey his own commandment, "Search the Scriptures." This is the reason and this the reward, "for they are they that testify of me." They testify of Christ. Yes, they are full of Christ. Rays from his cross shine through both the Testaments. Prophets and saints of old looked forward and rejoiced—"not having received the promises," it is true, "but having seen them afar off, and were persuaded of them and embraced them." Fuller, clearer light now shines on Calvary. Draw near and read again the sacred story. Yes, "search the Scriptures," for here you will surely find Jesus. His love prompted every promise, and is the pledge and fulfillment of every promise.

Seek him in the place of social prayer. Thomas was not at the prayer-meeting when Jesus manifested himself to his disciples. How much he lost by staying away! When Jesus draws near and says, "Peace be unto you!" then let me be within hearing of his gentle voice. Let me be near when he says, "Receive ye the Holy Ghost." *Only* a prayer-meeting," do you say? *Only* a visit from Jesus, the Giver of peace! Who would miss a visit of so much profit—a visit of so much pleasure!

Seek Jesus at the sacramental supper. Jesus is there. There you may enjoy his longest, sweetest visits. There he speaks peace to his people. Sweet it is to meet Jesus in the closet; sweet visits there he pays his beloved and betrothed. Sweet it is to meet him in the holy Scriptures; sweet to find him in the place of social prayer. But sweeter far are his visits at the communion-table. To sit like Mary at his feet, to lie like John upon his bosom—was ever joy like this? was ever Jesus nearer? No longer do we say, "Saw ye Him whom my soul loveth?" We have found him! we have found him! "His left hand is under my head, while his right doth embrace me." I charge you, my unstable heart, that you forsake not, nor grieve again "Him whom my soul loveth."

Now that you have found him, cleave to him. "Abide in me," the Master says. In union with Christ the Christian finds his safety, strength and happiness. And the closer this union, the greater is the security, strength and happiness of the Christian. Would we be guided by his eye? Then must we be continually "looking unto Jesus." Do we need strength? "In the Lord Jehovah is everlasting strength." Are we seeking happiness? "Happy is he that hath the God of Jacob for his help, whose hope is in the Lord his God."

Cling closer, young Christian, cling closer to Christ. Learn to walk with him daily in sweet communion. Be not satisfied with an occasional visit from your Lord, but beseech him to abide with you. He is willing to come and abide with you. "If any man love me, he will keep my words: and my Father will love him, and we will come unto him, and make our abode with him."

II.

His Name.

"MY meditation of him shall be sweet" *when I remember his name.*

We need not say, as did Jacob, "Tell me, I pray thee, thy name." We know thy name, *Jehovah Tsidkenu*, "The Lord our Righteousness." We are all as an unclean thing, and all our righteousnesses are as filthy rags, and all the soap and nitre in the world cannot make us pure and holy. "If I wash myself with snow-water, and make my hands never so clean, yet shalt thou plunge me in the ditch, and mine own clothes shall abhor me." But in the covenant of the cross we come and change clothes with Christ. He takes our filthy rags and gives us his own spotless robe;

and we are "accepted in the Beloved," not having our "own righteousness, which is of the law, but that which is through the faith of Christ, the righteousness which is of God by faith."

We know thy name, *Jehovah Shalom*, The Lord of Peace. Sweet peace speedily follows as one of the results of justification. "And the work of righteousness shall be peace, and the effects of righteousness quietness and assurance for ever." Or, as the apostle expresses it in the Epistle to the Romans, "Therefore, being justified by faith, we have peace with God through our Lord Jesus Christ." Peace was one of the notes in the song which angels sung when He was born who himself "is our peace." And when he was parting from his disciples "peace" was among the last words that fell from his lips: "Peace I leave with you; my peace I give unto you." "Thou wilt keep him in perfect peace whose mind is stayed on thee." "Perfect peace," being interpreted, means, "Peace, peace." So that we shall have a double portion, "good measure, pressed down and shaken together and running over."

We know thy name, *Jehovah Nissi*, The Lord my Banner. "Thou hast given a banner to them that fear thee." He his own self is our standard and our standard-bearer, and we need not fear that our flag shall ever be taken, or that those who fight under it shall be beaten. Though we are but weak worms of the dust, and are called to contend "against principalities, against powers, against spiritual wickedness in high places," there is nothing more sure than that we shall win the day. "If God be for us, who can be against us?" Looking at the end from the beginning, and confident of victory, we can say, when buckling on the harness before the battle is begun, "We are more than conquerors through Him that loved us."

We know thy name, *Jehovah Rophi*,

The Lord my Healer. When he began his holy ministry here on earth, "Jesus went about all Galilee, teaching in their synagogues, and preaching the gospel of the kingdom, and healing all manner of sickness, and all manner of disease among the people." Some came to him groping in their blindness, others came on crutches, and many were carried to him on their beds; and he healed them all. Though he came from heaven mainly to heal diseases of the mind, yet while he labored here in the flesh he healed more diseases of the body. He is still the only Physician of the soul, and by far the best Physician of the body. "He knoweth our frame," this our mortal body, better than the wisest men, for he made it, and without his blessing the best prescription will do us no good. He is our Physician. When we are taken sick he is first called to our bedside. By prayer we lay hold of something at the mercy-seat that rings a bell in heaven, and he makes haste and comes down and "healeth all our diseases."

We know thy name, *Jehovah Jireh*, The Lord will Provide. He provided a lamb upon Mount Moriah for Abraham in his greatest emergency. He has also provided a Lamb for us—a Lamb without spot or blemish, "the Lamb slain from the foundation of the world." "Even Christ our Passover is sacrificed for us." On his guiltless head our guilt was laid. And having provided a Lamb for us, he will provide anything else. "My God shall supply all your need according to his riches in glory by Christ Jesus." As the greater includes the less, so the unspeakable gift embosoms all minor blessings. "He that spared not his own Son, but delivered him up for us all, how shall he not with him freely give us all things?"

We know thy name, *Jehovah Shammah*, The Lord is there. Wherever we may be called to go, the Lord is there. What strong consolation, what good cheer there is in this blessed truth,

> "Awake, asleep, at home, abroad,
> I am surrounded still with God!"

In every duty, in every difficulty, the Lord is there. In the lion's den and in the fiery furnace, the Lord is there. In sickness and in health, in sorrow and in joy, the Lord is there. When our pilgrimage is almost over, and we are going down into the dark valley, blessed be his name, we shall find that the Lord is there. "Yea, though I walk through the valley of the shadow of death, I will fear no evil, for thou art with me."

Beyond the valley there is a place about which we know very little; but we know that there is a house of many mansions, and we know that the Lord is there. "I go to prepare a place for you." There is a holy city along whose golden streets these feet shall one day walk; "And the name of the city from that day shall be, The Lord is there."

"Oh magnify the Lord with me, and let us exalt his name together." He is everything to us. Are we sinners? He is our Righteousness. Are we in trouble? He is our Peace. Are we soldiers? He is our Banner. Are we sick? He is our Healer. Are we in want of anything? He will provide. Are we going into eternity? He is there, waiting to receive us up into glory. "Oh magnify the Lord with me, and let us exalt his name together."

"My meditation of him shall be sweet" when I remember his name, for "they that know thy name shall put their trust in thee."

III.

The Assurance.

"MY meditation of him shall be sweet" *when I remember the assurance he has given me.*

To his dear children God is pleased to give earnests or pledges of the future bliss. We cannot think that any of the heirs of glory are wholly deprived of foretastes of heaven. Some indeed walk in the mist-clouds of doubt for a great part of their lives. Only at intervals the clouds part and reveal a ray of heavenly sunshine. They live amid clouds—it may be they die amid clouds—and never know clear shining until they reach the land of perpetual sunshine.

Others there are who pitch their tents upon "the high hill Clear." They live in the land Beulah, where the sun is ever shining and the birds are ever singing, where Giant Despair never comes and where Doubting Castle is not so much as seen. They live in the sunshine, they die in the sunshine—no, they do not die; they pass away, onward and upward, into clearer light and brighter sunshine. Light is sown for them on earth by Him who is the light of the world, and the harvest in eternity is abundant and glorious. The first-fruits here, though nothing compared with the after-fruits, are beautiful and greatly to be desired. Why may they not be enjoyed by all?

We hardly think it is God's will that his children should have a limited measure of peace and joy. Neither can we think it humility to doubt the words of our Lord Jesus: "I give unto them eternal life; and they shall never perish, neither shall any pluck them out of my hand."

"Yes," we hear you saying, "this is comforting for Christians, but am I a Christian? The clouds of unbelief often envelop me and exclude all heavenly light. 'Whereby shall I know that I shall inherit the land?' Who will assure me of my interest in Christ?"

"He that believeth on the Son of God hath the witness in himself." Can you remain ignorant of so great a change wrought within by the Spirit? Are there not many signs to prove to you that you are in Christ? Do you not believe and know that a change has passed over all your feelings and affections? Do you not love the things you once hated and hate the things you once loved? Do you not love all who bear the Saviour's image? Is not sin odious to you? Do you not find some pleasure in drawing near to God in prayer? Is not the thought of continuing in sin painful to you? Would you willingly grieve your Saviour?

We would not say, "Peace! peace!"

when there is no peace. We would have you look well to the foundations of your hope. Examine it closely. Let the light of the Word fall full and clear upon it. Look at it on every side, and rest not till you know that it is founded simply and solely upon the merits of the Redeemer. If you are sure Christ's work is really begun in your soul, you need have no doubt about its being continued and finally completed. The Master counts well the cost when he begins his work in the sinner's soul, and none shall ever mock his work, saying, "This man began to build and was not able to finish."

Having ascertained this all-important fact, you may be "always confident" till you enter his presence "with exceeding joy." You need not fear that you shall fall away. "Rejoice not against me, O mine enemy: when I fall, I shall arise." You shall be "kept by the power of God through faith unto salvation." You need never fear that

Christ will weary of his work, but you may be confident of this very thing, that he which has begun a good work in you will perform it until the day of Jesus Christ," and you shall stand "without fault before the throne."

We know some humble and sincere disciples will shrink back, saying, "We are not able," when we beg them to make Paul's language all their own. With their hands upon their mouths and their mouths in the dust, they dare not look up with perfect confidence; they think it almost presumption, or at least they say, despondingly, "It is not for me." "Paul," they say, "was an uncommon Christian—he attained a tall stature in holiness." So he did; and why? Because his was no half-way service; he gave no divided heart to his master. That was the reason why he so well understood the doctrine of full assurance. "If any man will do his will, he shall know of the doctrine." Do you understand these words of the Master? He does not say, "If any man fully keeps the law, which is the perfect will of the Father, he shall know of the doctrine," for it is not possible for any mere man perfectly to keep the commandments of God. Nor does he say, "If any man *does* the will," but, "If any man *will*"—is willing to do his will. If he shows a willing heart and mind, God will enlighten him more and more. And what is implied in this willing heart and mind but full consecration?

When shall we learn the secret of a happy life? "Ye cannot serve two masters." Those who give themselves up to Satan's service may lead an unhappy life, but greater must be the unhappiness of those who are trying to make a compromise between God and Satan. They can enjoy neither service; they are of all men most miserable.

O ye who have professed the name of Christ, come away from all inferior pleasures! Pleasures? They are not worthy of the name. One hour with Christ is worth them all. Will you then suffer them to hide the Saviour from your view?

Once we were happy all the day long, having given ourselves to Christ in the covenant of the cross. Christ was the source of our life, the fullness of our joy, all our salvation and all our desire. Having enjoyed his precious presence, we dreamed not that we could ever wander; we thought our hearts would cleave to him for evermore. We had no doubts in those days. "My Beloved is mine, and I am his," was the constant language of our heart. But, alas! the world again entered our heart, dividing it and leaving but half for God. Then came the clouds gathering thick and fast, till our Saviour was hidden from our view. Upon the ear of the watchman who went about the streets soon fell our mournful cry, "Saw ye Him whom my soul loveth?" We sought him, but we found him not.

Our gloom and grief increased. Oh for one hour of Jesus' presence! "Let all other joys forsake this heart," we cried, "if only we may again enjoy Jesus' presence." Feeling thus, we thrust the joys (falsely so called) of earth away, and kneeling at the mercy-seat, we renewed our covenant with Jesus. True, there was no joy in our hearts; we saw not yet his smile. But we could trust him where we could not trace him; so we confessed to him all our wanderings. We told him how we had thought to serve him with half our hearts, but now we would give him all. The first steps were taken in darkness, but God soon revealed his smiling face.

If this assurance is attainable by one, why not by all? If at one time it may be enjoyed, why not at all times? We have "for a foundation a stone, a tried stone, a precious corner-stone, a sure foundation," laid in Zion by the great Master-Builder.

Foundation-stones are chosen with great care and laid with care, for upon them the whole building depends. Look at this foundation-stone. Tell me, is it not perfect, sure and tried? This is the stone that the builders rejected: they perished, but it remaineth, and upon it the Lord hath built his Church. Believers in all ages and climes have built all their hopes of heaven upon it. Is it not a tried stone? Satan tried it and found no flaw; Pilate tried it and found no fault; the Father tried it and pronounced it good; and we have tried it and proved it so. What a sure foundation it is, with Christ for the corner-stone, the next stone faith, then repentance, hope, submission and all the graces! "Master, see what manner of stones are here." Are they not goodly stones? and will they not make a beautiful temple?

Upon Christ, the precious corner-stone, let us build our hopes of heaven, and dismiss all fears for the future.

My hope, my joy, my salvation, my desire, my righteousness, my strength, my all

—Christ in me "the hope of glory." "Lord, who shall abide in thy tabernacle? who shall dwell in thy holy hill?" I have not clean hands, nor a pure heart. Behold, I am vile. Nevertheless, I shall abide in thy tabernacle; I shall dwell in thy holy hill. Why? Because Christ is mine. His hands are spotless, his heart is pure, his righteousness is perfect. All his is mine, for he is mine. I build my hopes upon the Rock Christ Jesus. These hopes shall never be overthrown ; I have no fear of it.

When the head stone shall be placed I cannot tell, but I wait and work with joy, hoping unto the end. Sometimes weariness almost overcomes me, for building is hard work. Foes within and foes without make the labor exceedingly hard. But whether in joy or grief, the building goes on, and from the completed structure shouts shall ascend to the great Master-Builder: "Grace, grace unto it!" "Glory be to the Father, and to the Son, and to the Holy Ghost! Amen."

IV.

The Perfect Work.

"MY meditation of him shall be sweet" *when I consider his perfect work.*

What consternation must have been felt among the ranks of holy spirits when sin entered into the world, "and death by sin!" Could grief intrude into heaven, we should imagine *that* an hour of deepest anguish when the Father, looking down upon the fallen race, exclaimed, "How shall I pardon thee for this?" "How shall I put thee among the children?" How could the just and holy God justify the sinner? Not one of all the heavenly host could solve the problem. "How shall I give thee up?" burst from the heart of the loving Father. The beloved Son exclaims: "Deliver him from going down to the pit; I have found a ransom." "Who will seek and save these wanderers?" says the Father. "Father, send me," the Son replies; "I will seek them, and save them, and bring them home. I will bear the wrath due to them for sin; I will die for them." The Father accepts the Substitute; the Son lays aside his glory and girds himself for the mighty conflict. He looks along the line of weary years, and though he sees nothing but suffering, reproach and death, his holy purpose remains unshaken. The lost sheep of the house of Israel must be saved, and none but Jesus could save them.

"So he was their Saviour."

His work of *justification* is perfect. Look at it for a moment. What is justification? "Justification is an act of God's free grace, wherein he pardoneth *all* our sins, and accepteth us as righteous in his sight, only for the righteousness of Christ imputed to us, and received by faith alone."

Can there be anything more simple and beautiful and perfect than this? It is free to all; it is sufficient for all: "Whosoever will;" "And I will pardon *all* their iniquities." It is the work of a moment, but it abideth for ever. One look of faith, and life, eternal life, is yours.

"The moment a sinner believes
And trusts in his crucified Lord,
His pardon at once he receives,
Redemption in full through his blood."

His work of *adoption* is perfect. Like justification, it is done in a moment, and it abideth for ever. "Adoption is an act of God's free grace, whereby we are received into the number and have a right to all the privileges of the sons of God."

The Romans had a twofold form of adoption. The first was a private transaction between the parties, receiving the person adopted into the family; the second was the public recognition in the forum.

The moment we are justified we are

adopted. This is the private transaction. Hearing a voice from heaven saying, "Thy sins are forgiven thee; go in peace," we look up through our tears, and with rejoicing lips we cry, "Father!" "*Now* are we sons of God," placed among the children, because Jesus solved the mighty problem, showing how God can be just and yet justify the sinner. The public recognition will come very soon. When we reach the pearly gates, Jesus, our Elder Brother, will be waiting to receive and acknowledge us as his own. Standing before his Father and ours, he will stretch forth his hand toward his disciples and say, "Behold my mother and my brethren!"

His work of *sanctification* is perfect. It is not, like justification and adoption, an act done in a moment. It is a work slow and at times painful, yet sure and perfect. It begins when we are justified, it ends when we are glorified. "Sanctification is the *work* of God's free grace, whereby we are renewed in the whole man after the image of God, and are enabled more and more to die unto sin and live unto righteousness." It is often a painful work. "The flesh, with the affections and lusts," must be crucified. We must "die unto sin." The sound of the hammer and axe and iron tools is not heard by those who are without, yet every blow causes the heart to quiver, and the cutting is very painful. Nevertheless, who would not be "a carved stone" in the temple of our God?

We praise thee for this work, O God. We rejoice to know that thou wilt not weary of it, but wilt carry it on "until the day of Jesus Christ." We shall be perfect in that day. No imperfection shall remain in us—no sinful desire, no unholy thought. Jesus will say unto us, "Thou art all fair, my love; there is no spot in thee," and he will present us faultless before the presence of his glory with exceeding joy."

His work of *redemption* is perfect.

Christ, our Prophet, instructs us, "revealing to us, by his word and Spirit, the will of God for our salvation." Christ, our Priest, offers up himself "a sacrifice to satisfy divine justice and reconcile us to God." He also "maketh continual intercession for us." Christ, our King, subdues "us to himself;" he rules and defends us, and restrains and conquers "all his and our enemies." Is he not a perfect Redeemer? He redeems our souls from death, our bodies also from the grave. "My flesh also shall rest in hope," always confident of a glorious resurrection. "For I know that my Redeemer liveth, and that he shall stand at the latter day upon the earth; and though after my skin worms destroy this body, yet in my flesh shall I see God." "I will ransom them from the power of the grave; I will redeem them from death. O Death, I will be thy plague! O Grave, I will be thy destruction!"

Though some may cavil at this mystery

and say sneeringly, "How are the dead raised up? and with what body do they come?" yet we trust in the word of our God, and "*we know* that if our earthly house of this tabernacle were dissolved, we have a building of God, an house not made with hands, eternal in the heavens." Christ, "the first-fruits of them that slept," is risen; then how say some among you that there is no resurrection of the dead? "Christ is risen!" Oh glorious truth, first proclaimed to the women who came weeping to his sepulchre! "Fear ye not," the angel answered, "for I know that ye seek Jesus which was crucified. He is not here; for he is risen, as he said." Christ is risen! Then we which are Christ's shall rise also. "Because I live ye shall live also." "Behold, I show you a mystery:" "the dead shall be raised incorruptible, and we shall be changed. For this corruptible must put on incorruption, and this mortal must put on immortality."

O Lord, our Redeemer, Prophet, Priest and King, we praise thee for thy perfect work!

Yes, "my meditation of him shall be sweet" when I consider his perfect work. My Master too regards it with satisfaction; he sees of the travail of his soul, and is satisfied. His life on earth was sorrowful, but his triumph was complete. "Having spoiled principalities and powers," God's enemies and ours, "he made a show of them openly, triumphing over them in it," or in *himself*, as it may be rendered. As a victor returning from the fight, he ascended to the glory which he had with the Father "before the world was;" and the song of the glorified filled the high heavens with richer harmony as the Well-Beloved of the Father proved by the nail-prints that he had finished the work which was given him to do.

Coming ages will testify to his triumph and to the completeness of his work. On earth it was for the most part viewed not only with indifference, but even with unbelief and scorn. "He came unto his own, and his own received him not." "For a good work we stone thee not; but for blasphemy, and because that thou, being a man, makest thyself God." "He saved others; let him save himself, if he be Christ, the chosen of God." "If thou be Christ, save thyself and us." "If he be the King of Israel, let him now come down from the cross, and we will believe him." But now a mighty multitude swell the song, "Worthy is the Lamb that was slain, to receive power, and riches, and wisdom, and strength, and honor, and glory, and blessing. And every creature which is in heaven, and on the earth, and such as are in the sea, and all that are in them, heard I saying, Blessing, and honor, and glory, and power, be unto Him that sitteth upon the throne, and unto the Lamb, for ever and ever. And the four beasts said, Amen. And the four and twenty elders fell down and worshiped Him that liveth for ever and ever."

"Ten thousand times ten thousand sung
Loud anthems round the throne,
When lo! one solitary tongue
Began a song unknown—
A song unknown to angel ears—
A song that told of banished fears,
Of pardoned sins and dried up tears.

"Not one of all the heavenly host
Could these high notes attain,
But spirits from a distant coast
United in the strain;
Till he who first began the song,
To sing alone not suffered long,
Was mingled with a countless throng.

"And still, as hours are fleeting by,
The angels ever bear
Some newly-ransomed soul on high
To join the chorus there:
And so the song will louder grow,
Till all redeemed by Christ below
To that fair world of rapture go.

"Oh give me, Lord, my golden harp,
And tune my broken voice,

That I may sing of troubles sharp
  Exchanged for endless joys :
The song that ne'er was heard before—
A sinner reached the heavenly shore—
But now shall sound for evermore."

V.

The Chastening.

"MY meditation of him shall be sweet" *when I consider his chastenings*, for "blessed is the man whom thou chastenest, O Lord."

Of all the beatitudes this may appear to be the strangest. To the young disciple chastisements may seem anything but happiness; you see in them no beauty that you should desire them. If you have never been taught in the school of affliction, you cannot understand this; neither can you understand it if you have not learned well what you were there taught. Perhaps you have been greatly afflicted, and yet you can see no good fruits of it in your soul. Every disappointment has only increased bitter feelings in your heart. You are conscious of this. You are ready to say, "Where are the blessed effects of sorrow?" The Master comes "seeking fruit," and findeth none. Why is this? We reply, that sorrow in itself has no sanctifying power. Many are hardened by it, and rendered more unlovely and unholy. But the plane in the hand of the carpenter's Son cannot fail to make you better, and if you are not profited by it, it is because you do not rightly receive your sorrows.

While you were a stranger to the love of Christ you had no special consolation to sustain you in the time of trial. The consolations of God, which are neither few nor small, you had no right to appropriate. With every stroke of the rod you seemed to hear a terrible voice saying, "I, even I, will chastise you seven times for your sins." But now that you are reconciled to God, all is changed; you hear another voice saying, "As many as I love, I rebuke and chasten."

Henceforth, therefore, you may accept trials as love-tokens, for "whom the Lord loveth he chasteneth."

Perhaps, like Jonah, you have been sitting with great delight under the shadow of your gourd. To give you joy and comfort in the desert, God caused it to spring up. You felt glad and even thankful because of its pleasant shade, and while you rested under its shadow songs of praise ascended to the Giver. Yet "God prepared a worm." You woke one morning to find your beautiful gourd all withered. Never did the desert seem more dreary. You fainted under God's smiting, and with aching and rebellious heart you prayed for death. There seemed to be nothing for which to live, and you said, "It is better for me to die than to live."

"Doest thou well to be angry for the gourd?"

There are times when God shows his mercy to us by turning a deaf ear to our foolish prayer. No, I should not say he turneth a deaf ear to our prayer. He does hear, and he does answer, but not according to our asking. You asked death; he sent grace to live. "It is better for me to die," you said. God, by sparing your life, said most plainly, "It is better for you to live." God knows best.

If you are still mourning over your smitten gourd, permit us to give you some reasons why you should no longer mourn, or, at least, why you should not murmur.

Remember, the gourd was undeserved. You had done nothing to merit such a blessing. Perhaps even when it came it found you, like Jonah, indulging in bitter, reproachful thoughts. Wayward and wandering were you; loving and tender was God. Earthly parents bestow most tenderness and anxious thought upon the erring child. The Good Shepherd leaves the ninety and nine to search for the straying one. These things but faintly illustrate the dealings of God with his children.

Perhaps you were in the path of duty, and were not unthankful while you rested under the gourd. Still, you know that you deserve not the least of all God's mercies. Your sufferings are less than your sins deserve. "He hath not dealt with us after our sins, nor rewarded us according to our iniquities." "Wherefore doth a living man complain?" Let then this thought silence your complaints.

Remember also that the hand that smote the gourd was the hand of your Father, your loving Father. And this thought surely will give you comfort in your sorrow, and will even cause you by and by to sing aloud for joy. Knowing full well that "he doth not afflict willingly," you seek to know why he thus dealt with you. It ought to be enough for you to know that "*God* prepared a worm." "What I do thou knowest not now, but thou shalt know hereafter," should make us dumb before him, but so great is his condescension toward them that love him that he even tells them *why* the smiting was necessary. Your heart was fully set upon the gourd, and you were

> "Making a heaven down under the sun."

It may be that there was very little of the pilgrim spirit in your heart. The heart-tendrils were firmly fastened around the gourd; its uprooting seemed to rend you in twain. Bitter and severe was the pain, but the hand that dealt the blow is ready to bind up the bleeding wound, and in after days you will love to look upon this scar, for you will cherish it as a sweet reminder of God's faithfulness and mercy—not only as a monument, but also as a warning, for whenever you look upon it, it will say to you, "Little children, keep yourselves from idols."

Have you ever noticed the old grave-stones in some English burial-garden? The damp climate, which so soon obliterates the letters, has a kindly way of dealing with the horizontal stones. Into the deep grooves of the lettering little seeds are carried by the wind, and, lodging there, the dampness soon causes them to germinate, and in place of the blackness of decay spring up the characters in living green.

Into the deep scars caused by God's sharp instruments the precious seeds of divine consolation shall be wafted. Watered by your tears, they shall soon spring up, and in your sweet submission others will read your testimony to God's faithfulness: "I know, O Lord, that thy judgments are right, and that thou in faithfulness hast afflicted me."

When God uproots the gourd he gives us something better, and "our light affliction, which is but for a moment, worketh for us a far more exceeding and eternal weight of glory."

If Paul could call his calamities "light," surely we may; for what are our trials when compared with his? Behold what a crushing load he carried! "In labors more abundant, in stripes above measure, in prisons more frequent, in deaths oft. Of the Jews five times received I forty stripes save one. Thrice was I beaten with rods, once was I stoned, thrice I suffered shipwreck, a night and a day I have been in the deep, in journeyings often, in perils of waters, in perils of robbers, in perils by mine own countrymen, in perils by the heathen, in perils in the city, in perils in the wilderness, in perils in the sea, in perils among false brethren; in weariness and painfulness, in watchings often, in hunger and thirst, in fastings often, in cold and nakedness." Oh what a life! How could he call all these afflictions light? Placed in the balance with the exceeding weight of glory, they seemed as naught. The afflictions were but for a moment; the glory was eternal.

"Many are the afflictions of the righteous, but the Lord delivereth him out of them all. He keepeth all his bones: not one of them is broken. Evil shall slay the wicked: and they that hate the righteous shall be desolate. The Lord redeemeth the soul of his servants; and none of them that trust in him shall be desolate."

Then "wait on the Lord; be of good courage, and he shall strengthen thy heart: wait, I say, on the Lord." And let your meditation be sweet when you consider Him who smites the gourd in order that he may lead you to the shadow of the great Rock.

"When my heart is overwhelmed, lead me to the Rock that is higher than I."

VI.

The Compassion.

"MY meditation of him shall be sweet" *when I remember his compassion* for the multitude.

It was a beautiful thought to compile a record of loving and heroic deeds, of all lands and ages, and to entitle it, "A Book of Golden Deeds." Florence Nightingale, whose picture adorns the opening page, stands forth a fit exponent of the spirit of love that prompted these recorded acts.

The record of Christ's life may truly be called "A Book of Golden Deeds;" and that blessed name, which is above every name, becomes the symbol of "whatsoever things are lovely and of good report." The works which mark his earthly career are wonderful beyond compare, and the crowning act of this life of perfect self-abnegation is the greatest mystery of love.

It was noble in Dick Williamzoon, the Netherland martyr, when safely over the frozen mere, to turn back, at the peril of his life, and rescue his pursuer, whom he saw about to perish in the waters. He saved his enemy, and was himself captured and burned at the stake—a martyr for mercy as well as for truth. It was nobler still in the Moravian missionary to enter the hospital in order to preach Christ to the lepers. "If you go in, you can never be allowed to come out." "I accept," he said, and entered, to go out no more. But the compassion of Jesus towers far above the devotion of mortals, and expresses itself in a manner which excites wonder in heaven and upon earth. Looking down from his heavenly throne, his heart was deeply affected by the ruin of our race. One blow of the arch-destroyer had marred God's fair creation—man. Could no hand restore what in one dark hour had been lost? O mighty Restorer! we wonder and adore.

> "He left his lofty throne,
>   And threw his robes aside;
> On wings of love came down,
>   And wept and bled and died."

Yes, girding himself with full strength, he descended to the work his loving heart devised. Humbling himself to bear our sins, he became our Saviour. Not satisfied with simply bearing the sins of his people, he also carried their sorrows, and so becomes their Sympathizer. "Surely he has borne our griefs" as well as our guilt. He became "a Man of Sorrows" in order that from henceforth and for ever his followers might have not exemption from all sorrow, but a Saviour who would be able to sustain them fully in their afflictions, even lifting them so far above their sorrows that at midnight and in prison they might sing praises.

Gazing along the line of centuries, the omniscient Jesus saw a mighty multitude of bowed and suffering ones—in sickness, in pains, in poverty and chains; inheritors of "cruel mockings and scourgings, yea, moreover, of bonds and imprisonment;" those whose portion should be to be stoned, "sawn asunder," tempted, "slain with the sword;" who should wander about "in sheep-skins and goat-skins, being destitute, afflicted, tormented." Seeing these, is it any wonder if his heart melted with tenderness? In the simple story of his life we read: "And Jesus went forth and saw a great multitude, and was moved with compassion toward them, and he healed their sick." "In all their affliction he was afflicted." Blessed be our High Priest who is still "touched with the feeling of our infirmities!"

When his life on earth ended and he returned to the glory which he had with the Father before the world was, he left us an example that we should walk in his steps. To his disciples belongs the honor of taking up and carrying forward the work of ministration. Partakers of Christ's love and sympathy "look not every man on his own things, but every man also on the things of others. Let the same mind be in you which was also in Christ Jesus," who "took upon him the form of a servant." "He that saith he abideth in him, ought himself also to walk even as he walked."

How did he walk? Study well the memorial of "golden deeds." Compare your life with his. How can you bear the test?

Nothing can be more beautiful than a life of self-abnegation. One single act of devotion to another's good is like a ray of golden sunshine in a darkened room, and a life of such deeds may well be called a golden life. Into the cabin of one of our government transports was borne a poor wounded soldier, who, with many others, was going home to die. He had just been laid in the middle berth—by far the most comfortable of the three tiers of berths in the ship's cabin—and was still thrilling with the pain of being carried from the field, when he saw a comrade in even greater suffering than himself about to be lifted to the berth above him, and, thinking of the pain it would cost him to be raised so high, he exclaimed, "Put me up there; I reckon I'll bear hoisting better than he will."

Where can we find sufficient inspiration for a life of devotion to others? "Act as if the eyes of Cato were always upon you," was urged upon the Roman youth to stimulate him to virtuous deeds. Act as if the eyes of Jesus were upon you, we urge, for surely he bends from his throne to watch you as you endeavor to tread the path your Saviour trod.

To some of us God has given leisure from arduous toil, wealth, talents and many opportunities for usefulness. Perhaps to all these gifts he has added strong faith and bright hopes of heaven. What, then, are our duties to the poor and ignorant, the weary and feeble ones? "Strengthen ye the weak hands and confirm the feeble knees. Say to them that are of a feeble heart, Be strong; fear not." Remember, and forget it not, ye favored ones, that "unto whomsoever much is given, of him shall much be required." Let nothing be hoarded. "Withhold not good from them to whom it is due, when it is in the power of thine hand to do it." Nature's and the Gospels' doctrine is, "Be ready to distribute, willing to communicate." Looking up at the twelve silver statues in Yorkminster cathedral, Oliver Cromwell asked, "Who are those expensive fellows up there?" He was told that they were the apostles of Christ. "Ah? let them be taken down and melted up," said the old Puritan; "then they, like their Master, will go about doing good."

It is said that in China the rich buy up

and distribute clothing to the poor, and in times of scarcity of food, through the kindness of the rich, rice is sold to the poor at a third or fourth less than the market price. This is done to win the favor of the gods. While we do not hope to purchase God's favor by anything that we can do, yet we may remember the words of the Lord Jesus, how he said, "Whosoever shall give to drink unto one of these little ones a cup of cold water only, in the name of a disciple, verily I say unto you, He shall in nowise lose his reward." "And they that be wise shall shine in the brightness of the firmament, and they that turn many to righteousness, as the stars for ever and ever."

Let us daily strive to imitate our Master in compassion for others; then shall our meditation prove profitable as well as pleasant.

VII.

The Sympathy.

"MY meditation of him shall be sweet" *when I remember his sympathy* with his chosen ones.

To have a friend who is ready to rejoice with us when we rejoice, and to weep with us when we weep, how delightful it is! It doubles our every joy and divides our every sorrow. Though some hearts seem to scorn this tender plant of heavenly origin, we believe that none are wholly insensible to the magic power of sympathy. Those who scorn it most are often led to crave it most when the days of bitter grief draw near. We call it a plant of heavenly origin, and so it is; for though it is often found in unrenewed hearts, yet it attains its fairest perfection in hearts regenerated by the Holy Spirit. Planted by the hand of God and watered by heavenly dews, it reaches its greatest height, and wins the admiration of many who fail to understand the secret source of its life.

But human sympathy, even the deepest and tenderest, often fails us in the hour of our greatest need. Who will say that Peter and the two sons of Zebedee were not friends of the Lord Jesus? Certainly they loved him, for they followed him whithersoever he went. Feeling his need of human sympathy—for he was the man Christ Jesus—he took them with him to Gethsemane. All he asked was that they should watch with him. "Tarry ye here, and watch with me." Did they watch? You know the record well. "And he cometh unto the disciples and findeth them asleep, and saith unto Peter, What, could ye not watch with me one hour?" When brought to our

Gethsemane, is not our experience something like our Master's? Where we looked for sympathy we find indifference; we are there alone. Perhaps our sorrow may be of such a nature that we cannot reveal it even to our best-beloved. Our secret grief lies like ice upon our hearts, sending its chilling influences through every member. The hands hang down listlessly and the feeble knees smite together; the aching of the head is only exceeded by the aching of the heart. Yet no one knows the agony that paralyzes our life. Or, sadder still, the heart-friend may be snatched away, and while our hearts are breaking by reason of bereavement, we may have no one left to whom we may turn for comfort in our affliction.

Is there no friend whose sympathy is deep, ever abiding and ever accessible? Thank God, there is One. His name is Jesus. In all our afflictions he is afflicted. He suffered that he might sympathize.

Coming to a race concerning whom it was written "few are their days and full of trouble," "it behooved him to be made like unto his brethren," therefore he accepted the inheritance of suffering, and became "a man of sorrows, and acquainted with grief." "Himself took our infirmities."

Is poverty your portion? Is it no uncommon thing for you to suffer hunger, cold and weariness? Do friends forsake and foes oppress you? Go and tell Jesus. Though no longer suffering the sorrows of earth, he remembers them well. Think you that *he* has forgotten those wilderness seasons when he suffered hunger; or those times of weary watching on the mountains; or that dark night when "all the disciples forsook him and fled;" or that sad hour when his Father forsook him? Though gone to God's right hand he is the same Jesus still. His heart is full of love and pity. "He knoweth our frame," for he has put on our humanity. He put on our humanity; he has never put it off. "Behold the Man!" "And I beheld, and lo, in the midst of the throne, and of the four beasts, and in the midst of the elders, stood a Lamb as it had been slain." "And I heard the voice of many angels round about the throne, and the beasts, and the elders; and the number of them was ten thousand times ten thousand, and thousands of thousands; saying with a loud voice, Worthy is the Lamb that was slain to receive power, and riches, and wisdom, and strength, and honor, and glory, and blessing."

And is he absorbed by this homage? I tell thee nay.

Let us recall that parting scene at Olivet. His days of suffering are now ended, and he is about to return to the glory which he had with the Father before the world was. A few words of parting, and then a cloud separates him from his sorrowing disciples. A cloud, the record tells us. So it appeared to them; to us it seems rather a company of shining ones—a heavenly convoy sent to attend King Jesus back to his heavenly throne. In the midst of the homage of this heavenly host he does not forget his sorrowful disciples, but arrests the glad song for a moment that he may send words of comfort down to them. "And while they looked steadfastly toward heaven as he went up, behold, two men stood by them in white apparel, which also said, Ye men of Galilee, why stand ye gazing up into heaven? This same Jesus which is taken up from you into heaven shall so come in like manner as ye have seen him go into heaven."

This same Jesus is not now absorbed by the homage of that "great multitude which no man could number." Surrounded by those "which came out of great tribulation," can he for a moment forget those who are going through great tribulation? He does not forget them. The hand that was nailed to the cross is still swift to obey the impulses of that great heart of love, and hastens to wipe away the tear that gathers in the mourner's eye, to bind up the broken heart and to smooth the pillow of the dying.

We cannot read the record of Christ's earthly life without perceiving that his sympathy with suffering was deep and constant. Failing to comprehend this, some may add to your grief by uttering these chilling words: "Trouble not the Master." Remember, and forget not the broken-hearted father whose "only daughter" died before the help of the Good Physician could be obtained. There comes one from the ruler's house saying unto him, "Thy daughter is dead; trouble not the Master." The mournful message is heard by the Master, and turning to the sorrowing father, he said, "Fear not; believe only, and she shall be made whole." How speedily joy came into that darkened home when Jesus entered and took the maiden by the hand!

Little know they that great heart of love who say to the sorrowful, "Trouble not the

Master." Young disciple, heed them not. Think no sorrow too trifling to pour into his sympathizing ear. Whatever troubles you interests him. "In all their affliction he was afflicted." No tear falls unnoticed by him; no sigh escapes unheard. He keepeth you "as the apple of his eye." What encouragement to carry your griefs to Jesus! Satan would suggest that we "trouble not the Master." He trembles to see such close communion between Christ and the Christian. He knows that his power over the Saviour's "hidden ones" is fast passing away, and he would be glad to raise all chilling barriers to their delightful intercourse. "Get thee behind me, Satan!" My Saviour invites, yea, urges, me to come to him with all my sorrows, and I will cast all my cares on him, for he careth for me. "It is good for me to draw near to God." Again and again have I found it good—oh how good! All sympathy is sweet, but his sympathy is exceeding sweet. Yes, so sweet is it that trouble is no longer trouble, because Christ shares it with me. He changes the "valley of Baca" into the "land Beulah." He gives me songs in the night, and his presence turns my darkness into day.

"Trouble not the Master."

I tell you, Satan, it is no trouble for the Master to care for me; no trouble to soothe my sorrowing spirit; no trouble to wipe away my tears; no trouble to pillow my aching head upon his bosom; no trouble to give me "beauty for ashes, the oil of joy for mourning, the garment of praise for the spirit of heaviness." Many and many a time has he done this, blessed be his name! Nothing troubles him but my sins. Would to God they might trouble him no more! They grieve him; then let me forsake them. By his help I will. Begone, unbelief, pride, worldliness, ingratitude—begone! It is ye that trouble my Master!

VIII.

The Love.

"MY meditation of him shall be sweet" *when I consider his love for me.*

The record of Christ's deeds of mercy toward a multitude of sick and suffering ones gives us a wonderful glimpse of his heart. The thought of his perfect sympathy with his people has comforted the Church in all ages. But draw a little nearer and consider his *personal love for you*, dear young Christian. Listen to his voice saying so tenderly, "I have loved thee." Forget for a moment the multitude that need his compassion and the disciples who share his sympathy, and try to realize his deep, personal love for you. Consider that love as shown on Calvary. Remember the great price he has paid for your redemption.

During the dark days of the Netherland revolt there went forth a decree from the cruel Philip the Second; and though many a bloody edict had gone out before from that throne, this one in cruelty exceeded them all, for it condemned to death all the inhabitants of the Netherlands. "Heretic" was branded upon every one, and, without respect to age or sex, they were doomed to destruction. Now, if a mighty deliverer could have traversed those gloomy streets proclaiming full deliverance for those who were condemned, with what joy would he have been hailed! Not only would the public thanks of the nation have been his, but each rescued one would have hastened to express his own thanks to his deliverer.

Let then your heart overflow with grateful love when you remember the great Deliverer. "Guilty" was branded upon every forehead when Jesus came to the rescue; and while the thanks of all the redeemed are ascending to the throne, let your praises unite with theirs, for you too were under condemnation when Jesus offered pardon. His terms were simple—"only believe;" and through the grace of God you were led to accept the offer of everlasting life. "There is therefore now no condemnation," for the Son hath made you free.

"No condemnation!" How sweet it sounds! How much it means! Christ hath fulfilled the Law's requirements, and you are free. As we meditate upon it we seem to hear the Saviour saying, "Lovest thou me?" Dear Lord Jesus, we cannot love thee as thou hast loved us. A mother's love is as naught when compared with thy love, for she *may* forget, but thou hast said thou wilt never forget us. But yet our hearts cherish most fondly this secret of thy love to us. "I have loved thee with an everlasting love."

It gives us joy in our loneliest hours. We love to think about it when we are all alone. Never are we less alone than when alone, for then it is we hear the sweetest whispers that ever fell on mortal ears. And when we hear the voice of our Beloved, can we be indifferent to his love? I tell thee, nay. Love, a faint reflection of his own, rises in our heart, and falling on our knees before him, we exclaim, "Lord, thou knowest all things; thou knowest that I love thee." Sadly we feel that it is a poor spark of love—nothing like his great love to us—yet we rejoice that the little spark is there, and pray that it may be kindled into a steady flame. "Lord, thou knowest all things." Oh how glad we are of this! Thou knowest every emotion of our heart toward thee. Thou knowest our grief because we do not love thee more.

But this meditation has its practical bearings. We may not always dwell upon the high mountain apart thinking about our

Saviour's love. Let our communion with Christ be as close and confidential as possible, but let us never forget that He who spent whole nights communing with his Father also spent whole days ministering to others. Let, then, the love of Christ constrain us.

Standing safely upon the Rock Christ Jesus, let our hearts go out in pity for those who are still breasting the billows. Faint and exhausted, they seem ready to perish. "Help, Master, help!" Let our prayers for them ascend unceasingly. The Master is not far off, and in answer to our prayers he will come and rescue them with his strong arm. Let the love of Christ constrain us to labor for the perishing around us. This is our working-time, and this principle of love is the life of our work.

This word "constrain" has several meanings. It might be thus expressed: "The love of Christ transports us." It carries away our souls in ecstasy even from earth to heaven, and fills us with holy rapture. How often at the table of the Lord have we been thus transported by thoughts of his everlasting love! And as we went on our pilgrim way we cast frequent glances back to that hour of heavenly brightness. Earth grew dim during those moments of holy communion. Fain would we have tabernacled there.

The love of Christ *urges* us, *prompts* us. Sweet it will be to rest in the arms of his love. But this rest remaineth; we have not yet reached it; to the present belong toil and labor. There must be no loitering in the Christian life. Where the love of Christ fills the heart there can be no loitering. It is a prompting principle, ever leading us to new endeavors for the Master.

The love of Christ *unites* us. Though diversities of opinion mark those who bear the Christian name, yet, if the Saviour's love fills our hearts, we have one common platform where we may meet and hold sweet fellowship. Our experience is the same: "we love him because he first loved us." Our Hope is the same: Christ in us, "the hope of glory." Our home is the same: "and there shall be one fold." Our Shepherd is the same: "and I will set up one Shepherd over them." And though our creeds may differ, our chorus is the same: "Thou art worthy, for thou wast slain, and hast redeemed us to God by thy blood out of every kindred, and tongue, and people, and nation." Angels and archangels round the throne join in the heavenly melody, saying, with a loud voice, "Worthy is the Lamb that was slain to receive power, and riches, and wisdom, and strength, and honor, and glory, and blessing." "And every creature which is in heaven, and on the earth, and under the earth, and such as are in the sea, and all that are in them," being united by the love of Christ, join in the song which celebrates his wondrous love.

IX.

The Life Abundant.

"MY meditation of him shall be sweet" *when I consider the life more abundant which he gives.*

We are amazed at the languid, feeble lives of many around us. Among the aged we naturally look for inactivity, but, alas! "even the youths" faint and are weary, and the young men utterly fall. Before "the time of old age" the grasshopper becomes a burden, and we hear the young exclaiming, in world-weary tones, "I have no pleasure in them." They said in their hearts, "Go to, now; I will prove thee with mirth; therefore enjoy pleasure." And behold they found it vanity. They builded houses, and planted vineyards, and gathered silver and gold; but, looking back on all the works their hands have wrought, they are compelled to acknowledge that all is vanity and vexation of spirit. Therefore they hate life and all their labor which they have taken "under the sun." "For what," say they, "hath man of all his labor, and of the vexation of his heart, wherein he hath labored under the sun? For all his days are sorrows, and his travail grief; yea, his heart taketh not rest in the night. This also is vanity."

How marked and beautiful the change when Jesus takes possession of these weary souls! "I am come," says the Master, "that they might have life, and that they might have it *more abundantly*"—life in greater quantity; "good measure, pressed down, and shaken together, and running over."

We hear much about the power of love to arouse the dormant faculties and animate the feeble spirit. When this love is the dear, deep love of Jesus, who can estimate its life-giving power? Truly, we hardly begin to live till Jesus reveals himself to us —until, kneeling at his cross, we consecrate to him our time, our talents and our all. From henceforth life has for us new beauty, because Jesus is the charm of our life.

Life "more abundantly!" Let us enter more deeply into the meaning of these words. Let us understand that religion does not close the door upon any lawful calling. The days of religious seclusion are long past, but the days have not yet come when men have fully learned that daily business is not antagonistic to Christian life, but that it is one of the means of its development. It has been truly said that there have been noble bands of Christians who have gone to heaven despising ambition, refusing crowns, disdaining sceptres, unwilling to be cumbered with wealth, willing to bear hardship and suffering; but there shall be another band of men who shall do more mighty things than they—men of higher grace who shall conquer enemies more strong and terrible, who shall go to heaven even with crowns and sceptres or with great wealth. Through abounding grace they learn Christian development in spite of, and by means of, those external things which cause the spiritual shipwreck of multitudes.

Let the spirit of the Saviour, dwelling in us richly, sanctify all commerce, all learning, all politics, all art. May religion dignify our every act. Religion was not simply designed for the dying hour. "Christ shall be magnified in my body, whether it be by life or by death." "For to me *to live* is Christ."

Dear Lord Jesus, thou hast showed me "the path of life," and by thy presence, even on earth, thou hast given me "fullness of joy." Thou hast given me power when faint, and "increased strength" when I had no might. Therefore my life shall praise thee. "A new creature" in Christ, henceforth I will not live unto myself, but unto Him which died for me and rose again, "for the love of Christ constraineth me."

X.

The Forgiveness.

"MY meditation of him shall be sweet" *when I consider the full and free forgiveness he imparts.*

The hour in which we first felt the joy of sins forgiven can never be forgotten. The burden had grown so heavy that we could carry it no longer, so, bending the knee at the foot of the cross, the burden was cast upon Christ.

For many days our joy and peace were so great that we fondly hoped to be burdened no more; but as old wounds often break out anew, so it is with the soul, and the memory of "sins that are past" often sweeps over the Christian like a bitter wave.

Daily sins cause daily grief to the heart that loves the Lord. The only way of peace is to carry them at once to Jesus, confess all and seek forgiveness. We never seek in vain.

But these past sins, these iniquities of our youth, how they rise up to condemn us and take away our peace! "Thou writest bitter things against me," saith Job, "and makest me possess the iniquities of my youth." "My sin is ever before me," cries David in the bitterness of his soul. It must have been a lifelong grief to Peter that he had denied his Lord and Master. Others might easily forget his hour of weakness and sin while they listened to his fearless words on the day of Pentecost and heard him exclaim, "Him, being delivered by the determinate counsel and foreknowledge of God, ye have taken, and by wicked hands have crucified and slain." But though others could forget, how often must Peter's soul have been saddened by the memory of his weakness and sin! Sounding along the corridors of memory, ever and anon these words, "I know not the man," must have smote upon his ears like a funeral knell. The recollection of that look of love must often have brought tears to his eyes and filled his heart with tender grief.

How many of us recall with deepest sorrow hours of weakness when, yielding to strong temptation, we fell into sin! Perhaps no eye but God's marked our wandering steps, no ear but his heard our words of sin, no heart but his read the dark secret. The hour of true contrition came when, ashamed and deeply grieved, we scarcely ventured to look up to our offended Father, but casting our tearful eyes upon the ground, we knelt and cried in anguish, "Thou hast set our iniquities before thee, our secret sins in the light of thy countenance." Remembering that "if we confess our sins he is faithful and just to forgive us our sins and to cleanse us from all unrighteousness," we freely confessed all, and in the deep peace that followed we found a fulfillment of the promise. "I acknowledge my sin unto thee, and mine iniquity have I not hid. I said, I will confess my transgressions unto the Lord, and thou forgavest the iniquity of my sin."

But though the Lord is "ready to forgive," and "plenteous in mercy" unto all them that call upon him, yet these past sins are weapons that the great adversary often uses successfully in his warfare with the pilgrims, causing many almost to stand still when they should be running in the way of God's commandments.

Think you that our God desires from us constant mourning over "sins that are past?" If these are to lie a perpetual burden on our hearts, robbing us of our peace and clouding our hopes of heaven, what advantage then hath the Christian? or what profit is there in the atonement of Christ?

We have somewhere heard of a chemist who was lecturing before his class. A number of rags of varied hue lay before him, and by means of strong chemicals he was changing their colors into whiteness. Presently he paused, and holding up a piece of Turkey red, he remarked, "Ah! now we shall have some trouble, for of all colors this is the hardest to extract." Again and again he dipped it into the strong solution, but with little effect; then cast it aside, saying, "It must either remain as it is, or else lie in the solution till its very fibres are destroyed."

But the blood of Christ has power to extract even scarlet stains. "Though your sins be as scarlet, they shall be white as snow; though they be red like crimson, they shall be as wool."

Then "why art thou cast down, O my soul?" for "the righteousness of God, which is by faith of Jesus Christ unto all them that believe," is "for the remission of sins that are past," as well as for the constantly recurring sins of the present.

Shall we, then, never think of our past sins? Yes; think of them as the mariner thinks of dangers past, and as the redeemed in glory think of past tribulations. "He maketh the storm a calm, so that the waves thereof are still. Then are they glad because they be quiet; so he bringeth them unto their desired haven." Yes; think of them with gratitude to God for deliverance, and let this be your song as you press on: "He sent from above, he took me; he drew me out of many waters: he delivered me from my strong enemy, and from them that hated me; for they were too strong for me." "When I said, My foot slippeth, thy mercy, O Lord, held me up." "The Lord is my rock, and my fortress, and my deliverer; the God of my rock: in him will I trust; he is my shield, and the horn of my salvation, my high tower, and my refuge, my Saviour." "For who is a God, save the

Lord? and who is a rock, save our God? Therefore I will give thanks unto thee, O Lord, among the heathen, and I will sing praises unto thy name."

Think of them, also, with humility and self-distrust, and let this be your constant prayer: "Hold up my goings in thy paths, that my footsteps slip not." "Keep me as the apple of the eye; hide me under the shadow of thy wings."

But oh do not carry the memory of past sins as a weight to drag your soul down to the dust! If the Lord has forgiven and forgotten them, why not rejoice in this wonderful token of his love toward you? Casting aside every weight, you may thus rise to the enjoyment of "a present heaven."

XI.

The Help.

"MY meditation of him shall be sweet" *when I remember the stones of help he has given.*

For forty days the champion of the Philistines had defied the armies of Israel. He was a man of great stature—a giant—and a man of war from his youth. "And all the men of Israel, when they saw the man, fled from him and were sore afraid." All, yet not all, for one accepted Goliath's challenge and stepped forth to battle with him. Who was he? The strongest, bravest and oldest veteran in the army? No; he was not a soldier, but a shepherd-boy, and too young to be enrolled. "A stripling" the king calls him, and his weapons are only "*five smooth stones!*" Is it any wonder that his elder brother chided him and that Goliath disdained him? Trusting in the Lord who delivered him out of the paw of the lion and out of the paw of the bear, he went forth confident of victory. He took a stone from his bag and put it in his sling, and buried it in the giant's forehead so that he fell prostrate to the ground. How wonderful!

There are giants still in the land—giant powers that defy the armies of the living God. There are giant sins and giant fears that throw themselves across the path of every Christian and threaten his destruction. And if this page shall meet the eye of some youthful warrior who would fain overcome those spiritual foes that challenge the soul, permit me to choose five smooth stones for you, with which you shall prevail to lay the giants low.

The presence of God is one of these stones: "Thou God seest me." Sometimes, like David's first stone, it is enough to kill the Goliath of temptation. When sinners entice us, there is power enough to defend us in the thought that the many eyes of the Most High are looking on us, and the soul starts back appalled, saying, "How then can I do this great wickedness, and sin against God?"

The power of God is another of these precious stones. David declined to go forth to battle with Saul's armor. He could not go with weapons which he had not proved, but he took to himself "the whole armor of God." He had proved it, and knew by experience that there was more than protection in that panoply. Goliath was a giant, but he was not God. He was mighty, but he was not almighty. He was potent, but he was not omnipotent.

The wisdom of God is still another of these stones. The mighty man of Gath was mailed from head to foot. He was completely covered with a coat of iron and brass. His whole body was protected; only his forehead was left exposed that he might be able to see his antagonist. And, strange to say, the first smooth stone went straight to this only place where it could harm him, "and sunk into his forehead." God's wisdom guided it to its own place.

The faithfulness of God is another of these stones. In his holy word he has made unto us many exceeding great and precious promises, and his faithfulness ensures their fulfillment. He will do as he said. Heaven and earth may pass away, but his promises shall never pass away. If ordinary means will not suffice for their accomplishment, miracles shall be wrought. The sun and moon shall stand still, if need be. Taking the past as pledge of the future, "there shall not fail one good word of all that the Lord our God hath spoken."

The love of God is the last stone of help. "And the last shall be first." It is the smoothest and most precious of the five.

There is some gold in all the others, but this one is all gold, and the most fine gold. In the presence, power, wisdom and faithfulness of God much love is mingled. He goes with us and upholds us and guides us and remembers his covenant because he loves us, so that our last thought crowns and comprehends all the others. The love of God is first and last and best. Presence, power, wisdom, faithfulness and love, these five ; but the greatest of these is love.

XII.

The Deliverance.

"MY meditation of him shall be sweet" *when I consider him as my Deliverer.*

How dense the gloom that gathers round the record of Adam's sin and fall! Reading this chapter without the cross before our eyes, it seems the saddest in all the inspired volume. Issuing from the abyss of woe, Satan has found an entrance into a newly-created world. Sin and death have bridged the gulf that separated earth from hell, and are swift to follow in Satan's track, eager to complete the ruin his hellish hate devised. Fiends from the pit rejoice, while angels, with grief-clouded faces, gaze upon the guilty pair. "Adam, where art thou?" Sinful man hears the summons, and, compelled by power divine, appears in the presence of his offended Maker. "Can any hide himself in secret places that I shall not see him? saith the Lord." "Though they hide themselves in the top of Carmel, I will search and take them out hence." Truly, "there is no darkness, nor shadow of death, where the workers of iniquity may hide themselves."

But when we read this record in the light of the cross, our grief speedily changes into gladness. That the promise made to Satan, "Thou shalt bruise his heel," has not been retracted, each disciple of Christ can testify. The old enmity hissed forth by the arch-apostate and his followers when the almighty Arm hurled them into their own place, has not yet been destroyed. The conflict, begun in Paradise, between the seed of the woman and the serpent—that conflict darkly shadowed forth in the mythology of heathen nations and painfully experienced by each regenerate heart—is raging still. "O wretched man that I am! who shall deliver me from the body of this death?" cries the Christian. "O my Father, if it be possible, let this cup pass from me!" prays the Christian's Lord and Master. That the bruising is not light, Gethsemane and Calvary bear mournful testimony. Nevertheless, it is not vital. Thou mayest bruise his heel, Satan, but not his head. From the abode of demons a yell of triumph must have risen when the Light of Life was extinguished on the cross. But the triumph was short-lived. "Rejoice not against me, O mine enemy; when I fall, I shall arise." "That which thou sowest is not quickened except it die." "Thou shalt bruise his heel" because Omnipotence allows it, for "it pleased the Lord to bruise him," but "it shall bruise thy head." "Traveling in the greatness of his strength," Jesus plants his feet upon the necks of his enemies and chains the captives to his triumphal car. The Lion of the tribe of Judah has seized the prey. "Judah, thou art he whom his brethren shall praise." "Let all the people praise thee, O God; let all the people praise thee." And those who will not render him willing homage shall be trampled under the wheels of his advancing chariot. "But these mine enemies, which would not that I should reign over them, bring hither, and slay them before me."

Shiloh, the Pacificator, has come; and though the conflict has not ceased, the combatants are already singing the conqueror's song. What meaneth this shout of triumph that cometh up from the battle-field? It is the voice of them that shout for the mastery. They go forth singing, "Thanks be unto God, which giveth us the victory, through our Lord Jesus Christ." We hear their song above the clash of arms; amid the smoke of the battle-field we see their look of quiet confidence; and as they fall in the conflict they shout, "O Death, where is thy sting? O Grave, where is thy victory?"

From heaven above is now proclaimed the blessing above the curse; and though Eden was lost through the disobedience of Adam, Paradise shall be regained through the obedience of Christ.

Mercy closed Eden's gate. "Behold, saith the Lord, the man is become as one of us, to know good and evil; and now, lest he put forth his hand, and take also of the tree of life, and eat, and live for ever, therefore the Lord God sent him forth from the garden of Eden." Life everlasting, even in the garden of Eden, would be no boon to a sin-stricken race.

The gates are open now not only "that the King of Glory may come in," but also for "the generation of them that seek him, that seek thy face, O God of Jacob." "They shall ascend into the hill of the Lord;" they "shall stand in his holy place."

XIII.

The Hearer of Prayer.

"MY meditation of him shall be sweet" *when I consider him as the Hearer and Answerer of prayer;* for his promises concerning prayer are many, making us always confident" when we come to the throne of the heavenly grace. Surely, every Christian may approach with confidence, saying in his heart, "My God will hear me." He may adopt the language of full assurance and say, "Father, I know that thou hearest me always." The Bible abounds in promises relating to prayer. We also find there many illustrations of God's willingness to answer the prayers of his children.

But some may say, "Notwithstanding the promises which appear so positive, we do not always receive that for which we ask." There are many reasons why this is so. Sometimes our motive in asking is wrong. "Ye ask, and receive not, because ye ask amiss." Sometimes we do not ask in faith, consequently, no answer comes; for thus reads the faithful promise: "All things whatsoever ye shall ask in prayer, *believing*, ye shall receive." Therefore "ask in faith, nothing wavering." There is another reason why we do not always receive the things for which we ask. In our ignorance and short-sightedness we often ask for that which God in his wisdom sees would be hurtful to us. Loving us with more than a mother's love, he withholds the evil which seems to us good, and sends the good which seems to us evil. Though God's providence may seem to contradict his promise, yet this is a faithful saying: "No good thing will he withhold from them that walk uprightly."

The wicked often prosper for a time. "They are not in trouble as other men; neither are they plagued like other men. Their eyes stand out with fatness, they have more than heart can wish. Behold, these are the ungodly who prosper in the world; they increase in riches."

How shall we solve this seeming contradiction? Suppose we cannot solve it. Shall we therefore arraign the justice of God? Shall we reject the promise because we cannot understand it in the light of God's providence? Oh, not so. Let us remember that now we know only in part. But do we not often forget the condition of this promise? Do we not make the promise void by our unworthy walking? "No good thing will he withhold from them that walk *uprightly*." "If ye abide in me, and my words abide in you, ye shall ask what ye will, and it shall be done unto you."

We must remember that God's standard of judging between good and evil is very different from ours. In this our thoughts are not as God's thoughts. We call poverty, sorrow, sickness and bereavement evil; God often shows us that they are good. We ask health; in answer God sends sickness, which he blesses to the healing of all our spiritual maladies. He can make our sick-chambers very Pisgahs, so that we shall thank him for sickness. Sometimes in our weariness and discouragement we pray for death. God in answer sends sufficient grace. He maketh our feet "like hind's feet," equal to the way. Is not his "a more excellent way?" It seems to us every Christian should be satisfied with answers like these. Is it not better to have our portion appointed by God? It is better when praying for temporal blessings always to say, in spirit if not in words, "Nevertheless, not my will, but thine be done."

There are some things for which you may ask without any limitations, and these are spiritual gifts; "for this is the will of God, even your sanctification." You may also have this confidence when praying for the conversion of friends. God has provided salvation sufficient for all. In our Father's house there is room enough, and in our Father's heart there is love enough, for all. None need perish with hunger. "As I live, saith the Lord God, I have no pleasure in the death of the wicked; but that the wicked should turn from his way and live." If, then, you have a desire in your heart for the conversion of a soul, be assured that God awakened that desire. It is a token of his readiness to bless. "Have faith in God," "and wait on thy God continually." Plead till the answer comes; "though it tarry, wait for it." "What things soever ye desire when ye pray, believe that ye receive them, and ye shall have them."

XIV.

The Reward.

"MY meditation of him shall be sweet" *when I think of his reward for faithful labor.*

The weariness of work is often very great, but if sufficient recompense follows our endeavors, if success crowns our working, we soon forget past toils, "for the desire accomplished is sweet to the soul." But if we can see no good resulting from our labors, disappointment and grief increase our fatigue. Yes, the weariness of grief far exceeds the weariness of successful labors, though they may be "labors more abundant," "in season" and "out of season." The faithful minister of Christ will here bear me witness, for of all times of exhaustion he will acknowledge this to be the greatest, when he goes from the pulpit to the closet with this despairing cry: "Who hath believed our report?" "Master, we have toiled all the night and have taken nothing."

It was morning when upon the shore of Tiberias three tired fishermen were seen. They were sad as well as weary, for the night had yielded them no recompense. From the crowd that pressed upon him to hear the word of God, Jesus stepped forth and entered into Simon's boat. And when he had left speaking, he said unto Simon, "Launch out into the deep, and let down your nets for a draught." Naturally enough, Simon, answering, said, "Master, we have toiled all the night." They were very tired now, and were greatly in need of rest and refreshment. "All the night." Slowly must the hours have worn away while they labored and waited. And then he added,

"We have taken nothing." We can almost hear the tone of disappointment in which he said it. It would have been no marvel if he had added, "Lord, if we have been so unsuccessful during the time that is generally the most favorable for fishing, will it not be useless for us to make another attempt? Besides, we are weary all over and almost sick with disappointment; let us at least wait till the falling darkness favors our work."

But Simon Peter's answer was marked by more faith than this. While he reminded the Master how long and unsuccessfully they had toiled, he quickly added, "Nevertheless, at thy word I will let down the net." And a great multitude of fishes was the result of this act of faith and prompt obedience. Peter and all that were with him were astonished at the draught of fishes which they had taken.

To our mind this astonishment does not confute the idea that this act of obedience was prompted by faith. The result so speedily followed, and was so great in its magnitude, that the strongest faith might well be taken by surprise. Have you not sometimes been surprised by the blessed and abundant answer to prayer which you have received? Perhaps the salvation of a dear friend was the deep desire of your heart. For this you toiled till you nearly fainted at the mercy-seat. You prayed unceasingly, and you believed it was the prayer of faith; yet when the answer came you were almost overcome with astonishment.

Contemplating this scene, let us take new courage. The sowing-time is often a time of exhaustion. It is also a time of weeping; from very weakness God's seed-bearers weep. The work is great; "who is sufficient for these things?" Sometimes God in his infinite wisdom sees fit to withhold from them the knowledge of the results they are really accomplishing. Often he calls them away before the seed is fully ripe, and they never see the harvest, nor hear the joyful song of the reapers who come after them. They sow in tears, and then they lie down at the close of the day, and with sighs and tears they pass away; but God watches over the precious seed, and the tear-watering causes it to flourish more abundantly and ensures a more glorious harvest. At the time of planting, if the husbandman sees no signs of coming rain, he steeps his seed over night in water that it may spring up sooner; but no seed springs up so soon as that which is steeped in tears. "He that goeth forth and weepeth, bearing precious seed, shall doubtless come again rejoicing, bringing his sheaves with him."

The present reward of work is very great, and much to be desired. "In all labor there is profit." Every deed done for the good of others brings a blessing to our own souls: seeking their happiness, we find our own. God's laborers are blessed above all others. He never forgets to reward the smallest work of love; even the cup of cold water given in his name shall be remembered. When we fail to accomplish the good we designed, we cannot say that our labors were in vain or that we have spent our strength for naught. God's designs have been accomplished; our souls have been disciplined; and as we sit down upon the ruins of our brightest plans and fairest hopes, we glorify God far more by our cheerful submission than we could have done by successful labors.

But the *future* reward, how great it is and how enduring! The harvest-time will be a time of joy. Past labor and weeping will be forgotten when the Lord of the vineyard shall call the laborers that he may reward them abundantly. What a scene will then be presented to our view! From north, from south, from east, from west, will they come—some who have toiled through the heat and burden of a long day; others who have labored but one short hour. I, too, will obey the call, saying, as I come and kneel before the God of the harvest, "Master, behold my sheaves. I know they are very few and of little worth; yet, Master, behold my sheaves." Then shall these cheering words come to me, and not to me only, but to all the faithful laborers: "Well done, good and faithful servant; enter thou into the joy of thy Lord."

Weary worker in the vineyard, waste not your strength in weeping. Say not, "I have labored in vain; I have spent my strength for naught, and in vain;" for surely your judgment is with the Lord, and your work, or your reward, with your God. "Thus saith the Lord, Refrain thy voice from weeping, and thine eyes from tears; for thy work shall be rewarded, saith the Lord."

XV.

The Soul's Portion.

"MY meditation of him shall be sweet" *when I consider him as my soul's best portion.*

Again and again in God's holy word are we warned to avoid covetousness. From the midst of the thunders and lightning of Sinai issues the emphatic command, "Thou shalt not covet." "Take heed, and beware of covetousness," saith the Master, "for a man's life consisteth not in the abundance of things which he possesseth." "Let your conversation be without covetousness," enjoins the great apostle, "and be content with such things as ye have; for he hath said, I will never leave thee, nor forsake thee."

In order, then, to gain this sweet content, let us meditate upon Christ, who is our soul's eternal portion. Let us consider what we already possess, and also meditate upon "things to come," till our hands shall relax their grasp upon earthly things and our hearts cling more closely to Christ. Our lips vainly declare, "Christ is all," if our lives contradict our lips. The worldling looks at our daily life, and soon judges whether or not we are satisfied with Christ.

"Conversation" means more than mere words. In its original meaning it includes the whole life. Our whole lives, then, must prove that Christ is our all.

Can we be contented in sickness, in sorrow and in poverty? Yes, we can; "for he hath said, I will never leave thee, nor forsake thee." In sickness the Lord will make all your bed; he will strengthen you upon the bed of languishing; his left hand will be under your head, while his right hand will embrace you. In sorrow he will be with you, for he has said, "When thou passest through the waters, I will be with thee; and through the rivers, they shall not overflow thee: when thou walkest through the fire, thou shalt not be burned; neither shall the flame kindle upon thee." In poverty be content, for though you are poor and, it may be, despised of men, you are not forgotten by God. That you might have eternal riches he became poor—so poor that he had not where to lay his head. The manger was his cradle and the rich man's tomb was borrowed for his burial. "For ye know the grace of our Lord Jesus Christ, that, though he was rich, yet for your sakes he became poor, that ye through his poverty might be rich."

Christ is our *eternal* portion, "for he hath said, I will *never* leave thee, nor forsake thee." "Lo, I am with you alway" were his last words on earth. Be content, then, with such things as ye have. Having Christ, ye possess all things, "for all things are yours; and ye are Christ's, and Christ is God's."

The "things present," which belong to us through the covenant of peace made with Christ, are precious and greatly to be desired. We have the promise of all things needful for this life. "My God shall supply all your need." "No good thing will he withhold from them that walk uprightly." Bread is sure; water is sure. "The young lions do lack, and suffer hunger; but they that seek the Lord shall not want any good thing." "Therefore I say unto you, Take no thought for your life, what ye shall eat, or what ye shall drink; nor yet for your body, what ye shall put on." "Consider the ravens" and "the lilies," and "be not faithless, but believing;" for if God so feedeth the ravens and clotheth the lilies, "how much more will he" feed and clothe you, "O ye of little faith!"

Come and meditate upon his promises, for they are positive and sure, and full of sweet comfort. All your wants are supplied by your Lord Jesus. Are you sick? He is your Healer. Are you weary? He is your Rest. Are you in trouble? He is your very present Helper. Are the days dark? He is your Sun. Are you in danger from the darts of the adversary? He is your Shield. Does the desert sun beat hot upon your head and the desert sand scorch your pilgrim feet? He is "as the shadow of a great rock in a weary land." When the wicked, even your enemies and your foes, come upon you, he is your Fortress and your strong Tower. He is your Teacher, Brother, Friend and Saviour. What more do you desire?

And when "things present" are about to pass away for ever, and your trembling feet touch the cold waters of the river of death, before the last fond grasp of earth is given, Christ will take your hand in his, and as he draws very near to you, you will feel in that hour that Christ is the best portion your soul can possess. His finger will point plainly toward "things to come," and he will doubtless give you glimpses of glory before the time.

We need not, however, wait till the last hour to consider the things God has laid up for us. The lesson of present content is more easily learned while we sit, like Bunyan's Patience, waiting for our good things. Passion would not be satisfied till his lap was filled with golden treasure, but Patience, with empty hands, was very quiet, though Passion laughed scornfully. "Patience," says Bunyan, "is willing to wait."

What a beautiful figure of the Christian! And what are these good things for which the Christian is willing to wait?

First of all, he has a home in the future. No earthly home can be compared to it, for it is a home where change and death never come. The earthly home may be made desolate by death, but in the heavenly home there shall be no vacant place. "There shall be no more death, neither sorrow nor crying, neither shall there be any more pain; for the former things are passed away."

The Christian has also a crown laid up in the future. Here thorns may bruise his aching brow, but there he shall be crowned. And earthly crowns will pale before the Christian's crown of glory. If he is wise in winning souls, they shall be placed as jewels in his crown; for though all will have bright crowns, some shall be surpassingly glorious, being studded with immortal souls.

Let me, dear Lord, be one of those who "turn many to righteousness." Give me a glorious crown, and I will gladly lay it at thy feet. No matter if it must be with weeping that I now go forth to win souls, no matter if my heart be weary and my hands be heavy, the reward will more than compensate for the weariness and weeping, and every redeemed soul shall shine in my diadem of glory.

Let the worldling keep his portion and

clutch his paltry treasures till they crumble to dust beneath his eager fingers, but let

> "My soul to heaven aspire,
> And fix its all on God."

He is my best portion, and "my meditation of him shall be sweet" when I remember that this "good part," which his grace has enabled me to choose, "shall not be taken away" from me.

XVI.

The Cross.

"MY meditation of him shall be sweet" *when I consider his cross and mine.*

The cross is the emblem of our religion. To it the awakened sinner flies when conscience fills him with gloomy fears. There is no place of safety for him save in its blessed shadow. Looking up with faith, he sees Jesus, the suffering Saviour, and with the sight peace and joy fill his heart. As he starts upon his pilgrim course the cross is set before him, and these are his marching orders: "If any man will come after me, let him deny himself, and take up his cross, and follow me." Oh how he learns to love that cross of shame! it becomes radiant with glory, and as he journeys he sings,

"In the cross of Christ I glory."

As he bears his own personal cross, which sometimes is exceedingly heavy, he lays the heaviest end of it upon Christ, and looks up joyfully through his tears to the great Cross-Bearer and learns to "glory in tribulation." Looking up, what does he see? Beyond the cross he sees the crown. How dazzling! how enduring! No stain nor rust shall ever mar its beauty; none shall ever rob it of its sparkling gems.

Tell me, I ask, who shall wear these bright crowns? "And he said unto me, These are they which came out of great tribulation, and have washed their robes, and made them white in the blood of the Lamb." Out of great tribulation into great exaltation. What a striking contrast! What a happy exchange! Like the Master, they passed from a lowly state of trouble into a lofty state of triumph. Because they were not ashamed of him in his grief, he was not ashamed of them in his glory. They were saved not because they suffered, but because they trusted in Him who suffered for them. Some of them suffered even unto the death, but the blood that made white their garments was not their own; it was "the blood of the Lamb." "*Therefore* are they before the throne of God, and serve him day and night in his temple: and he that sitteth on the throne shall dwell among them."

How happy are they now! Former trials, when recalled, only lead them to new songs of praise. They remember all the way of the past, and strike the harp-strings with exultant fingers when they think of their sufferings, now exchanged for endless joys.

Consider your cross, young disciple, and meditate upon it without bitter thought. It was a wise and loving Hand that laid it upon your shoulder, and that same Hand will lift it when he thinks you have carried it long enough. "He doeth all things well." The end shall be better than the beginning, and in eternity you will understand it all. Your voice will rise in higher, loftier strains when you remember the sickness that was sanctified and the sorrow that led you nearer to your God.

"Oh what a load of struggle and distress
Falls off before the cross! The feverish care;
The wish that we were other than we are;
The sick regrets; the yearnings numberless;
The thought, "this might have been," so apt to press
On the reluctant soul; even past despair;
Past sin itself,—all, all is turned to fair,
Ay, to a scheme of ordered happiness,
As soon as we love God, or rather know
That God loves us! . . . Accepting the great pledge
Of his concern for all our wants and woe,
We cease to tremble upon danger's edge;
While varying troubles form and burst anew,
Safe in a Father's arms we smile as infants do."

XVII.

The Presence.

"MY meditation of him shall be sweet" *when I remember his near and constant presence;* for he is the joy of my life and the life of my joy. Joy without him is hardly worth the name of joy, and sorrow with him is better than joy.

When my heart is overwhelmed because of enemies and foes, my terrified soul turns quickly to him, and David's prayer becomes all my own: "Be not thou far from me, O Lord; O my Strength, haste thee to help me! Deliver my soul." The answer quickly comes: "Wait on the Lord; be of good courage, and he shall strengthen thine heart."

But oh, my Saviour, "they mar my path." Remove these enemies, even for thine own name's sake; for then shall I run in the way of holiness and my ever-brightening path shall show forth thy praise.

And again the answer comes: "Commit thy way unto the Lord;" "My presence shall go with thee."

Nearer and nearer draws the Saviour; sweeter and sweeter is his presence in this time of my soul's sorest need. He lifts my prostrate soul and bids my weary eyes survey the upward path. How glorious to behold! He tells me "these light afflictions" are working out "a far more exceeding and eternal weight of glory." And when I feel his strong arms around me, my soul breaks forth in singing:

> "I have no foe, with thee at hand to bless;
> Ills have no weight, and tears no bitterness."

Blessed is the man who has learned the secret of a happy life, and, like Enoch, walks with God. We care not to know the outward circumstances of him whose inner life is hid with God. His delighted soul bathes in the sunshine of God's smile; his face reflects the peace that flows like a river through his spirit.

It was the presence of Christ that made the Emmaus journey so delightful. We know that the favored two started with slow steps and heavy hearts, and there was a deep undertone of sadness in their voices as they talked together of all the strange things that had happened. But what a change came over them! A stranger joined their company, and as he talked with them their hearts burned within them, till, drawing near the journey's end, they felt so unwilling to lose his company that they constrained him to come in and tarry with them. And so it came to pass that the last hours of the day were the best hours. In the morning it was cloudy and dark, but at evening-time it was light, for as they sat at meat the Sun of Righteousness shone full and clear into their hearts, dispersing all the clouds.

Does not this journey remind us of some of the days of our pilgrimage? The morning found us heavy-hearted. We knelt at the mercy-seat, while sighs and groans took the place of songs and rejoicings. With slow steps and aching hearts we began the duties of the day. But soon there came a change. Jesus, our Lord, drew near. He spake some cheering promise, uttered some whisper of his love. Our hearts began to melt; again we knelt at the mercy-seat. We prayed, we praised; we rose and hastened to our duties, singing as we worked; and so the hours sped on. Night fell; still he tarried: we slept in sweet security, for "so he giveth his beloved sleep;" we woke to find that we were still with Jesus.

Happy the soul that hath the abiding presence of the Saviour. Be this our constant prayer: "Abide with us." "Lord, I am not worthy that thou shouldst come under my roof," but yet my heart cries out, "Abide with me." Give me light in the evening-time. Abide with me "until the day break and the shadows flee away."

"Not a brief glance I beg, a passing word,
But as thou dwell'st with thy disciples, Lord—
Familiar, condescending, patient, free—
Come, not to sojourn, but abide, with me."

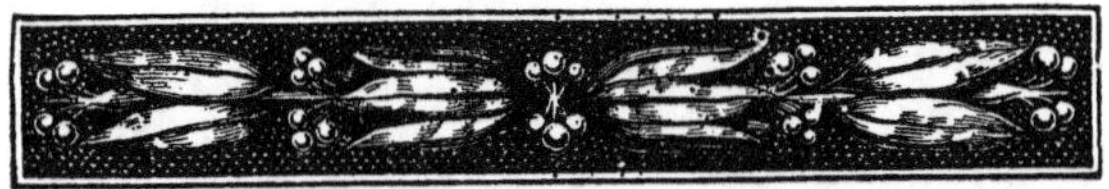

XVIII.

The Appearing.

"MY meditation of him shall be sweet" *when I consider his appearing.*

To those who have refused the Saviour's offer of mercy the thought of his second coming is full of terror. With them there is a "certain fearful looking for of judgment and fiery indignation." Having "trodden under foot the Son of God," and "counted the blood of the covenant wherewith he was sanctified an unholy thing," is it any wonder if they fear to fall into the hands of the living God, knowing full well that the fearful and unbelieving "shall have their part in the lake which burneth with fire and brimstone?"

But the event which strikes such terror into the hearts of those who are without Christ and without hope in the world, fills the heart of the Christian with exceeding joy. There is comfort, yea, great comfort, in the thought of Christ's coming. The apostles departed from Olivet with new hope and joy after receiving this angel message: "This same Jesus which is taken up from you into heaven shall so come in like manner as ye have seen him go into heaven." Ever since, the waiting Church has been gazing steadfastly toward heaven, "looking for that blessed hope, and the glorious appearing of the great God and our Saviour Jesus Christ." And ever and anon angel voices have uttered words of comfort to the waiting ones. Often the voice is the voice of our Beloved, the Angel of the Covenant. "I will come again," he says, "and receive you unto myself; that where I am, there ye may be also." Hear his last prayer: "Father, I will that they also, whom thou hast given me, be with me where I am; that they may behold my glory." Hear the last words of inspiration: "Surely I come quickly." And the waiting company of believers joyfully respond, "Amen. Even so, come, Lord Jesus."

The thought of his coming comforts those whose dearest friends sleep in Jesus, for them will God bring with him. This shall be a time of glad reunions. Let us not sorrow "as others which have no hope." We shall soon be ever with one another."

There is deliverance in the thought of Christ's coming; "for we that are in this tabernacle do groan, being burdened." Yes, young disciple, we have not yet reached that state of perfection when we have no burdens. We are yet in the body, and the burden of sorrow is often upon us; and though we try to cast this burden on the Lord, we yet look forward with joy to Christ's coming, for then "sorrow and sighing shall flee away," and "God shall wipe away all tears." And though Christ has delivered us from the penalty of the broken law, yet the burden of sin is often upon us, and many times with contrition and shame we bow before the mercy-seat, saying, sadly, "Father, I have sinned against heaven and in thy sight, and am no more worthy to be called thy son." The burden of death is upon us, and Christ's coming gives comfort to those who through fear of death are all their lifetime subject to bondage.

Trembling disciple, perhaps you are fearing what may never come upon you. You may be among the number of those who shall be alive at the coming of the Lord. The time may not be distant, for nearly all the prophecies have been fulfilled and the signs of the times seem to declare plainly, "The coming of the Lord draweth nigh." Many a time, it is true, the waiting Church has fancied it heard the sound of his chariot-wheels, but the time was not yet.

"Where is the promise of his coming?" cries the scoffing world. "Behold, I come quickly." Believers closely clasp this promise to their hearts while they pray for patience to wait. Generations have passed away, but the word of the Lord endureth for ever. "I come quickly." Perhaps this generation shall not pass away till all be fulfilled. It may be so. Certainly there is "upon the earth distress of nations, with perplexity;" men's hearts are "failing them for fear, and for looking after those things which are coming on the earth."

"My Lord, I stand continually upon my watch-tower," remembering the benediction, "Blessed are those servants whom the Lord when he cometh shall find watching."

Last of all and best of all, *there is glory* in the thought of Christ's coming. There is comfort, great comfort; there is deliverance, great deliverance; there is glory, great glory, "a far more exceeding and eternal weight of glory." "Behold, I show you a mystery; we shall not all sleep, but we shall all be changed, in a moment, in the twinkling of an eye, at the last trump; for the trumpet shall sound, and the dead shall be raised incorruptible, and we shall be changed; for this corruptible must put on incorruption, and this mortal must put on immortality. So when this corruptible shall have put on incorruption, and this mortal shall have put on immortality, then shall be brought to pass the saying that is written, Death is swallowed up in victory." What a glorious picture! No doubt is here admitted. "We *shall* be changed;" "this corruptible *must* put on incorruption;" "this mortal *must* put on immortality."

This thought of glory overwhelms us; it is a "weight of glory." To be ever with one another is blessedness; to be ever with the Lord is glory. To be free from this body of sin and death is deliverance; to wear the likeness of our glorified Lord is transfiguration—wonderful, dazzling, glorious!

Is it any wonder, then, if our meditation is sweet when we reflect upon "the glorious appearing of the great God and our Saviour Jesus Christ," "who shall change our vile body, that it may be fashioned like unto his glorious body, according to the working whereby he is able even to subdue all things unto himself?" No wonder the apostle calls it "a blessed hope." It sustains the heart of the aged Christian who has "fought a good fight" and finished his course. It also helps the young disciple to "run with patience" the race that is set before him.

"This same Jesus shall come again." How? "In like manner as ye have seen him go into heaven." "Behold he cometh with clouds," and with "ten thousand of his saints." And why does he come? To take his weary children home. "I will come again and receive you unto myself."

"Wherefore, comfort one another with these words."

XIX.

The Conclusion.

"LET us hear the conclusion of the whole matter."

We have meditated upon the names of Christ, and have found in them a sweet significance. Jehovah Tsidkenu satisfied the demands of the broken law, making us righteous in the sight of God. Jehovah Shalom gave a peace which even this tumultuous world cannot take from us. Jehovah Nissi leads us forth to battle against our mighty foes, and always gives us the victory; "thanks be to God!" Jehovah Rophi healeth all our diseases with marvelous skill: even the broken heart is not beyond his power, for his own word de clares, "He healeth the broken in heart, and bindeth up their wounds." Jehovah Jireh quiets all our fears for the future, for his name is sufficient pledge that he will supply all our need. Jehovah Shammah completes and crowns our joy, for in his presence is fullness of joy; "his presence is salvation."

We have rejoiced in "the earnest of our inheritance." Glimpses of glory before the time have made us homesick. His "perfect work" has filled our minds with amazement as we meditated upon our adoption, justification, sanctification and redemption. The thoughts of his chastenings were not painful, because we knew a blessing was concealed in the blow. His compassion for the multitude seemed to us a sweet thought; but as we learned something more about his sympathy with all his "sanctified ones," and his deep personal love for each individual Christian, our hearts melted within us, and drawing nearer to this great heart of love, we joyfully exclaimed, "This is my Beloved, and this is my Friend, O daughters of Jerusalem."

We have considered the life more abundant which he gives, until life with Christ seemed the happiest life man can know. Thoughts of the full and free forgiveness of all our sins, even sins of scarlet hue, were comforting thoughts; and while we cast the past behind our backs, we looked forward to the future with new confidence, remembering the "stones of help" provided by him to slay the giant sins. Deliverance from the curse was certainly a pleasant thought; and as we gazed into Paradise regained, we gave thanks because Christ had purchased for us the "right to the tree of life" which stands in the midst of the Paradise of God.

Our meditation was sweet when we thought of his faithful promises concerning prayer, for his word confirmed our own experience, and we learned to kneel and ask with a more unwavering confidence. Considering his reward for faithful labors made us almost forget the weariness of work as we seemed already to hear his "Well done, thou good and faithful servant; enter thou into the joy of thy Lord."

Christ as the soul's best portion filled the heart with deep, unspeakable joy, and we took up our cross, singing as we walked, because his near presence made us almost unmindful of its weight upon our shoulder.

On Olivet we had our last glimpse of our living Lord. Here we stood "gazing up into heaven" at "this same Jesus," who is as dear to us as he was to the twelve. Our hearts thrilled over his parting blessing, and the thought of his coming again filled us with delight.

Our meditations are over now. They have been "sweet," or, as it may be rendered, "as the calm evening hour." Meditating upon Jesus has increased our joy: "I will be glad in the Lord." Around his very name sweet thoughts thickly cluster. Jesus! my Jesus! In that dear name the best music of heaven comes down to me.

How sweet it sounds! A bundle of myrrh it is—a hill of frankincense—a mountain of spices. Through all the live-long day, through all the silent watches of the night, my mind may turn to Him whose "name is as ointment poured forth," and no bitter, doubting, fearful thought shall ever mingle with my musing. No dark thread shall ever weave itself into the silver web of my sweet meditation of him, for my unbelief is banished when my Jesus is near. All my grief fades away in the presence of his glory, and he his own self is the joy of my heart and the heart of my joy.

"My Beloved is mine, and I am his." All that he is is mine, and all that I am is his. He is more than all the world to me, and without him heaven would not be worth having. "Whom have I in heaven but thee? and there is none upon earth that I desire besides thee." Jesus! my Jesus! Eternal musings will not exhaust this hive of honey. He has saved me from my sins and betrothed me to himself for ever. O my soul, "how much owest thou unto my Lord!" The greatness of my indebtedness I will not fully realize till I stand upon the yonder shore, and perhaps not even then.

> "Jesus, I ne'er can pay
> The debt I owe thy love."

I am, and ever will be, "debtor." Thy gifts to me have been so great that, though my giving cannot enrich thee, I would fain relieve my grateful heart by giving thee some token of love.

In the stable at Bethlehem the Eastern sages open their costly treasures. The sight is a strange one, and there seems a strange incongruity between the gifts and the receiver; also between the giver and the receiver. The wise men bow before a babe, and lavish the riches of the East upon the infant of the lowly manger. "Lavish," did I say? Let not the thought of waste be here implied. This babe is "the holy child Jesus," the King of the Jews. Bring costly sacrifices. "The kings of Tarshish and of the isles shall bring presents; the kings of Sheba and Seba shall offer gifts. Yea, all kings shall fall down before him; all nations shall serve him."

Jesus, Saviour, once a child! Jesus, my exalted King! what shall I bring to thy footstool? What shall I give my Lord?

"Were the whole realm of nature mine,
That were a present far too small."

But I am poor, very poor. No good works have I to bring; no incense of holy prayers; no golden thoughts in which there mingles no alloy of impurity.

"Thou willest that thy bride should be—
I bless thy will—most poor, most low,
Receiving everything from thee,
My Lord and God. Then be it so.

"That I have nothing of my own,
Freely and gladly I to all declare.
This is my portion, this alone,
That thou permittest me thy name to bear."

Have I then nothing to give? Stay, holy Christ; I have a heart. True, it is polluted—more than this, it is broken—yet I have heard that though

"Our God requires a whole heart or none,
Yet he will accept a broken one."

Accept the gift. Take it and make it holy; fill it with love to thee. Fill it even to overflowing; so that, having received all from thee, I may be able to give thee all. Let me be wholly thine—thine in every thought and passion of my soul. Here, Lord, I give my soul to thee; I am thine.

"Poor heart of mine, awake, arise!
And thou, my Bridegroom, my life's Sun,
Draw me to reach the heavenly prize,
Oh, do thou draw, and we will run.
Draw after thee thy fainting bride,
Who still is far, too far, from light and grace;

> Till in thy presence, at thy side,
> She see thee wholly—see thee face to face."

My meditation of him makes me long to see Him whom, having not seen, I love. I would see him—not as I have seen him in the sanctuary and in his holy supper, but I would see him "face to face." I would see him as he is; and, blessed be his glorious name for ever! I shall one day see him thus. Oh blessed hope! These eyes shall see Jesus; "For I know that my Redeemer liveth, and that he shall stand at the latter day upon the earth; and though after my skin worms destroy this body, yet in my flesh shall I see God; whom I shall see for myself, and mine eyes shall behold, and not another."

And, better than all beside, I shall be like him; for "we know that when he shall appear we shall be like him, for we shall see him as he is." Such knowledge is too wonderful for me: it is high; I cannot attain unto it.

"Jesus! the very thought is sweet;
In that dear name all heart-joys meet;
But sweeter than the honey far
The glimpses of his presence are.

"No word is sung more sweet than this;
No name is heard more full of bliss;
No thought brings sweeter comfort nigh
Than Jesus, Son of God most high.

"Jesus, the Hope of souls forlorn,
How good to them for sin that mourn!
To them that seek thee, oh how kind!
But what art thou to them that find!

"No tongue of mortal can express,
No letter write, its blessedness:
Alone who hath thee in his heart
Knows, love of Jesus, what thou art.

"O Jesus! King of wondrous might;
O Victor! glorious from the fight;
Sweetness that may not be expressed,
And altogether loveliest."

THE END.

www.ingramcontent.com/pod-product-compliance
Lightning Source LLC
LaVergne TN
LVHW021408110826
845150LV00007B/1835